*For Jelena, my grapefruit, mom, dad,
and all bunnies in the world—Anton*

Mina, Kian & Milo—Anne

Explore the Rainforest

Emma and Louis in the Jungle

Written by Anne Ameri-Siemens
Illustrated by Anton Hallmann
Translated by David Wilson

LITTLE GESTALTEN

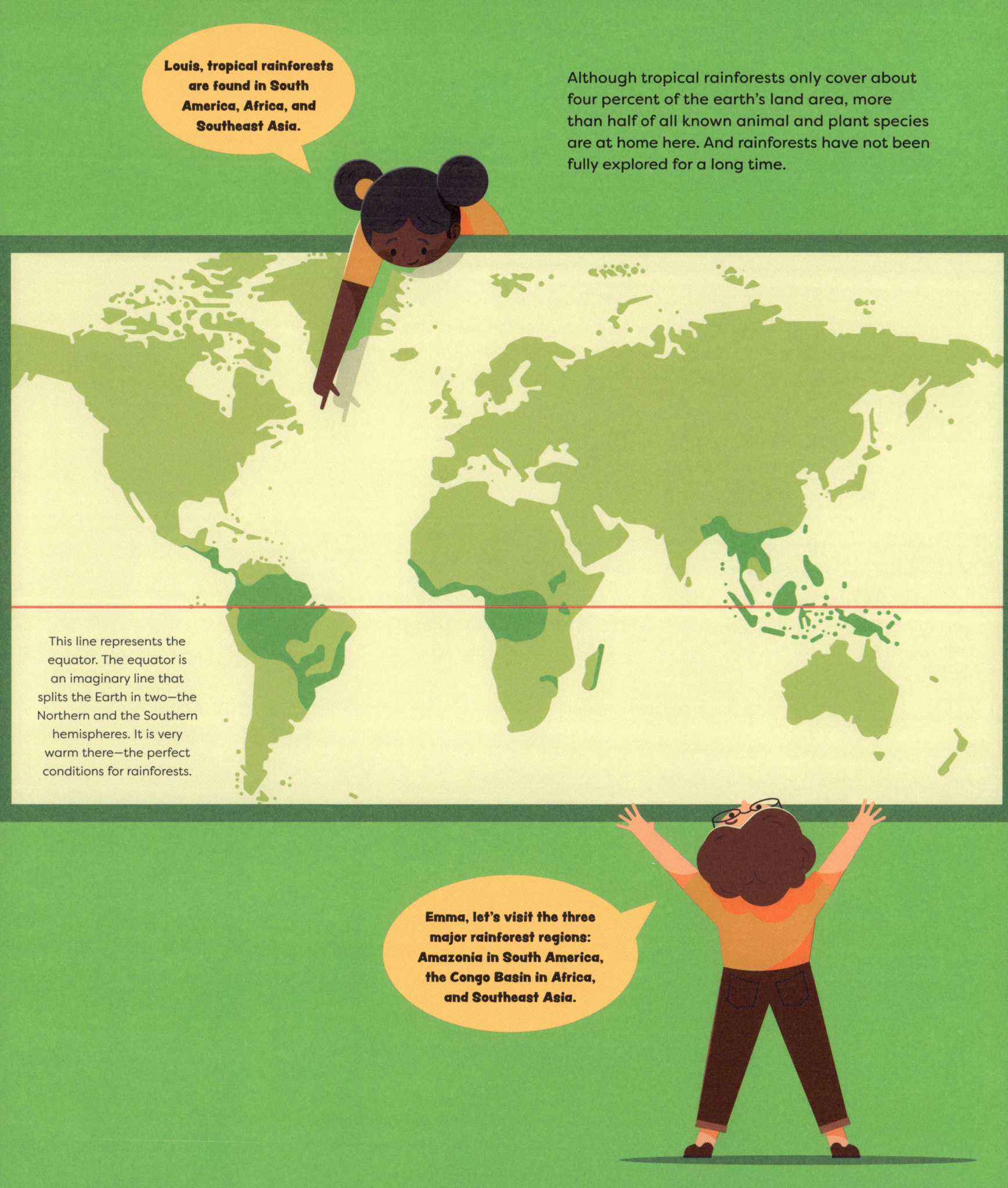

Off to the Rainforest!

Emma and Louis find it hard to decide where to look first! They're surrounded by the most amazing animals! Venomous frogs with bright yellow and blue skin croak, jaguars nap up in the branches of the trees, and ants, beetles and locusts swarm all around them. Butterflies flutter here, and monkeys are swing there from tree to tree on the vines.

The tropical rainforest is like a green universe of its own. Lots of different animals live here, along with countless types of plants like ferns, orchids, banana plants, and gigantic trees.

Anyone who wants to go on a nature study tour must first get used to the very moist air. This makes it quite hard to breathe. It's also warm—to say the least! And of course it rains a lot. That's obvious from the name "rainforest". Emma and Louis soon accustom themselves to the climate, and they just love exploring the rainforests. The biggest of all are in Africa (the Congo Basin), South America (the Amazon), and Southeast Asia. And they're starting off in Africa.

Come with us on a journey of discovery!

What is the Rainforest?

Tropical rainforests are found along the equator. Because it rains regularly throughout the year and is warm, the plants grow quickly here. But they are all in competition for nutrients and light.

How can you recognize a rainforest?

- It is always warm—the temperature in the summer is hardly any different from in the winter
- Rainforests are always green—though some of the trees do lose their leaves, they do it at different times of the year so it will always appear green
- It rains regularly throughout the year and the air is always moist
- Plants and trees grow at different levels
- There are lots of animals and plants in tropical rainforests that don't exist anywhere else in the world! These species are called endemics
- Rainforest plants are mainly pollinated by animals and not by the wind
- While forests in Europe and the USA also contain many different varieties of animals and plants, the fact that hundreds of them might live on a single tree is unique to the rainforest

Unique variety

On one hectare of rainforest you might find up to 280 different types of tree. A hectare is the equivalent of almost one and a half soccer fields.

Creepy crawlies everywhere ...

More than half of all known animal and plant species are believed to be living in the rainforest. Scientists have discovered no less than 100,000 species of insects.

Why does it rain so much?

1. As it's so hot, a lot of water evaporates in the rainforests. Near the equator, where the tropical rainforests are located, the power of the sun is very intense and it heats the ground.

2. As the water evaporates and moves upwards, it forms water vapor which cools off and condenses, forming into clouds. These clouds grow until they have large amounts of rain.

3. Plants and the soil absorb this moisture in a process known as "the small water cycle". The drops of water fall as rain, bringing water back to earth.

5. The evaporated water doesn't fall only on rainforests. The wind also carries the clouds away to provide rain for regions further away.

4. During one year in the Amazon rainforest, a single square yard of land will accumulate enough rainwater to fill 14 bathtubs.

Rainforests store so much water that they influence the climate of the whole world!

Rainforests and the World

Why are rainforests so important?

Humans and animals all over the world need the rainforests. The trees and plants store large quantities of carbon by absorbing carbon dioxide (CO_2) from the air. They use the carbon for their own growth and this produces oxygen, which all of us need in order to stay alive. The South American rainforest is often called "the lungs of the earth" because of the amount of oxygen it produces. Protecting the rainforests is vital for all of us.

Why is it so important that everyone in the world is a little different?

The variety of life

In recent years there has been a lot of discussion about stopping humans from cutting down the trees of the rainforest. They do this for various reasons—for instance to sell the wood, to create grazing land for cattle, or to plant useful crops. But every tree is important as it provides a home for numerous insects, spiders, snakes, birds, reptiles, amphibians, and mammals.

The variety of life in an area is what we call biodiversity. Members of one species can have very different abilities to members of another, and they don't all look exactly the same. Maybe you've got a pet? If you compare it to someone else's pet, you'll see that every individual animal is different. Some species are able to deal with changes in the climate or the environment, or with illnesses better than others. And so variety within a species can enable them to survive different crises.

What's on the menu?

Do you think you have eaten anything from the rainforest? You've probably tried quite a lot! Avocados, mangoes, pineapples, bananas, and papayas grow there—among other things! A lot of these things all taste nice and some can even help you a little if you're feeling unwell—like a tea that can be made out of papaya blossoms to help you deal with a cough. Cocoa, cinnamon, ginger, and vanilla also come from the rainforest.

In some countries, insects are eaten as snacks or served in restaurants.

The Structure of a Rainforest

In a rainforest, plants and animals have their homes at different levels—it's a bit like a skyscraper. But some inhabitants of the jungle also move between floors.

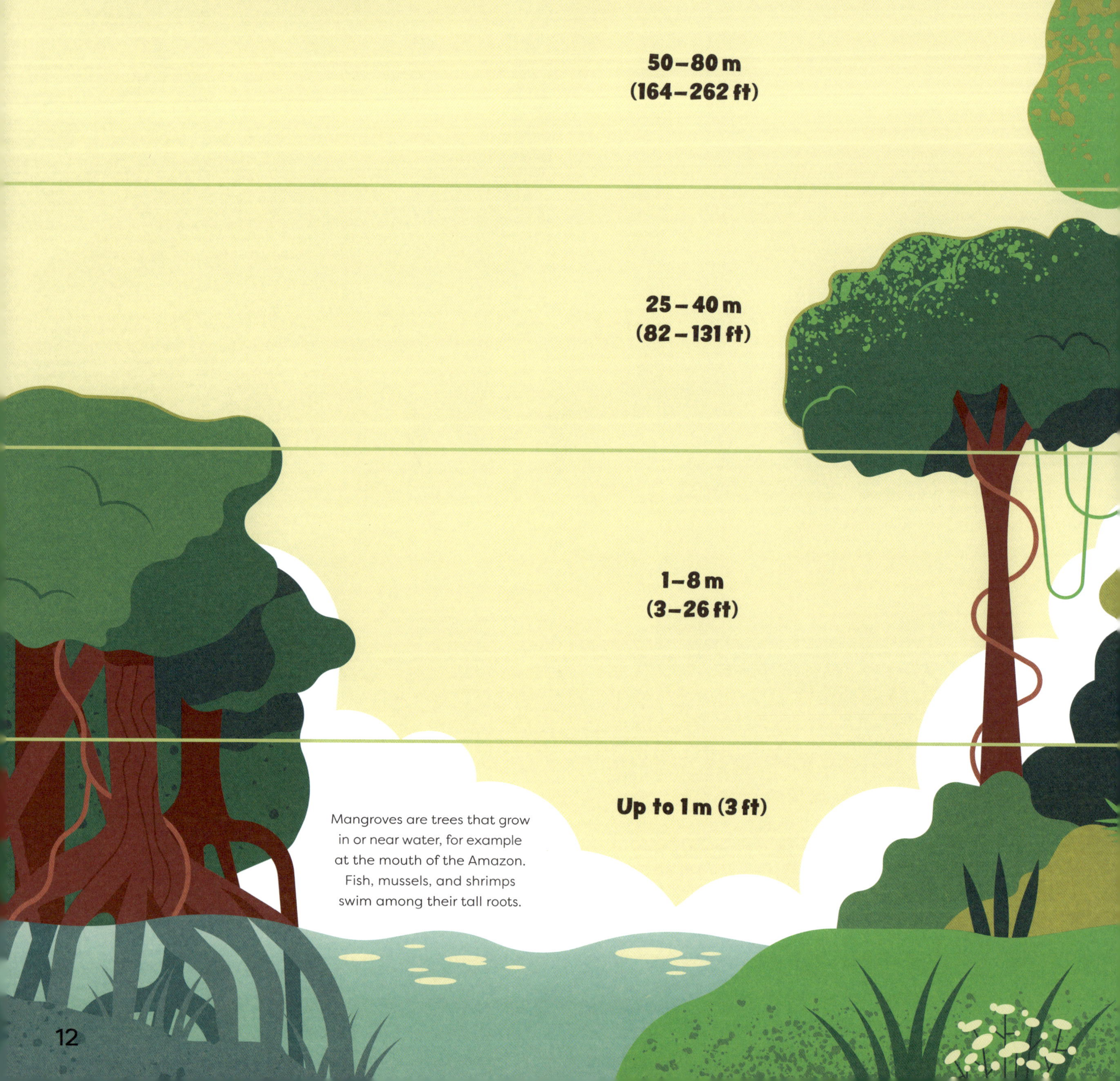

**50–80 m
(164–262 ft)**

**25–40 m
(82–131 ft)**

**1–8 m
(3–26 ft)**

Up to 1 m (3 ft)

Mangroves are trees that grow in or near water, for example at the mouth of the Amazon. Fish, mussels, and shrimps swim among their tall roots.

Each layer of the rainforest receives a different amount of sunlight and rain.

Emergent Layer

Kapok and Brazil nut trees tower above the canopy. These giant trees have special roots which only go a little way underground and instead spread all round the trunk like thick buttresses. There is a lot of sunlight up here as well as animals like monkeys, parrots and butterflies.

Canopy Layer

At this level, the leafy canopy receives plenty of sunshine and rain. Throughout the year, there are lots of buds, leaves, nuts and berries—much to the delight of the monkeys, bird and sloths that feed on them.

Understory Layer

Small rodents and snakes live among the bushes, shrubs and flowers. They receive regular visits from the higher levels. Jaguars, for instance, come to hunt smaller mammals, and humming birds suck nectar from the flowers.

Forest Floor

This is the home of fungi, small plants and of course lots of insects and spiders. Crocodiles, lizards and some mammals also feel at home here. So close to the ground, the air is especially moist, and owing to the thick canopy of leaves, the floor of the forest is quite dark.

The Rainforest in Africa

The African rainforest—the first in the world—was formed millions of years ago, when the land surface of the Earth was still a single continent.

Dinosaurs in the rainforest?

In those days, there were not nearly as many different animals and plants as there are now. Scientists have learnt that through fossilized leaves. The canopy was not as thick then. The dinosaurs died out around 66 million years ago, when a meteorite struck the Earth. Many of the species that live on the Earth today gradually evolved from the life left on Earth after this catastrophe.

The leaves of many jungle giants are covered with a layer of wax that protects them from the sun.

The Congo River is over 4,700 km (2900 mi) long.

Madagascar is the only place on Earth to find lemurs. Over 30 different species live there!

Much to discover

The second largest rainforest is in the Congo Basin. It covers an area of approx. 202,000 sq km (78,000 sq mi), which is larger than the US State of Alaska. Only the Amazon rainforest is bigger. In the Congo Basin there are more than 10,000 species of plant, 400 of mammals, and 1,000 species of birds.

A crocodile can reach speeds of up to 30 km (18.5 mph) per hour. That's faster than an e-scooter!

The Congo

The Congo River flows through the middle of Africa's tropical rainforest. Hippos and crocodiles bask on its banks. But beware, they are lightning fast in the water! Many exotic fish live in the underwater world of the Congo. In some places the river is so deep (220 m / 720 ft!) that so far only a small part of the water world could be explored.

Manatees have inhabited the earth for 50 million years. The African manatee spends most of the day underwater grazing and sleeping.

Research in the rainforest

A lot of what we know about the rainforests is thanks to brave and curious researchers. Through their efforts, we know about the rich biodiversity and about what properties plants and animals have. Did you know that chimpanzees can remember something for a lifetime?

?

Area:
3 million sq km
(1.158 million sq miles)

People:
Indigenous peoples such as the Aka, Baka, Mbuti, Twa, Batwa and Mbendjele have unique knowledge of nature.

Special features:
The deepest river in the world—the Congo.

Exceptional animals:
gorillas, forest elephant, African manatee, okapi.

Unusual plants:
Dragon's blood tree, spotted ferns.

British primateologist, Dame Jane Goodall is the world's foremost expert on chimpanzees. She began to study them in the 1960s.

Zoologist Diane Fossey founded a research station to find out more about gorillas. She was also very committed to the protection of gorillas.

Indigenous people in the African Rainforest

People with different languages and cultures have lived in the rainforest for centuries. They al have one thing in common—their close ties with nature. One of the groups that live in the rainforest is the Batwa.

What is day-to-day life like?

The Batwa hunt traditionally with bows and arrows, and gather herbs, fruits, and honey. The older generations pass their knowledge on to their children, teaching them how to find food, and what plants will help them if they fall ill.

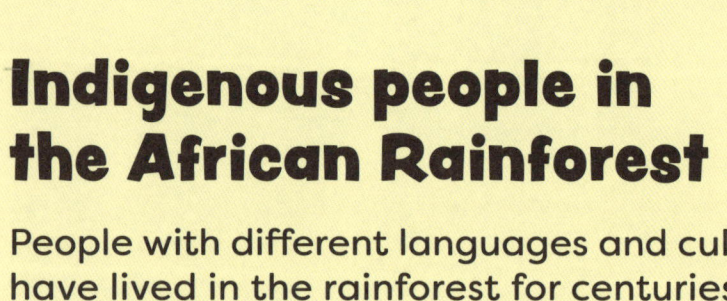

The Batwa wear different cloths which they wrap around their bodies.

The Batwa can recognize and classify animal tracks. This is very useful when they go hunting, or to warn them if they are going in the same direction as a dangerous predator. Today's scientists believe that there are now comparatively few people left in the rainforests that lead the traditional life of the hunter gatherer.

What sort of family life do they have?

A Batwa family consists of a wide circle of people—not just parents and children, but also grandparents, uncles and aunts, and their children. Their huts are made of dried grass and wood, and their tools are also made of wood. In the rainforest, families use whatever materials they can find in order to preserve their traditional way of life.

There are more than 5,000 indigenous groups in the world.

Protecting the Batwa

For a long time, there was no respect for the Batwa and their culture. They and other indigenous groups were deprived of their living space by people from the outside. In recent years, however, some African states have passed laws that recognize and protect indigenous people and their cultures.

?

What does indigenous mean?

"Indigenous" is the word used to describe the original inhabitants of a country or region. These are the first people to have lived there. Other examples of indigenous people include the Maoris in New Zealand and the Inuits in Alaska.

The Rainforest Floor

In the humid warmth—far from sunlight—there is a great variety of plants. Animals find plenty of food here.

Okapis

The dark fur and striped legs of okapis are the perfect camouflage between bushes and trees. Their tongue is so long that they can not only pick buds and fruits with it—they can reach their eyes with it! Handy when you want to scare away insects.

Brush-eared pigs

They are cunning omnivores that follow the sounds of monkeys and birds to find fruit. With their snouts, brush-eared pigs also plow through the earth for tubers and roots. This is good for the rainforest ecosystem. Many plants can germinate in the loosened soil.

While a human baby takes months to crawl and then walk, okapi cubs are on their feet shortly after birth.

The rainforest supplies itself

Dead plants or plant parts fall to the ground.

Fungi in the soil decompose them.

Healthy nutrients are released.

Plants absorb these nutrients through their roots.

This cycle of soil fungi and the roots of a plant is called mycorrhiza.

Getting around

Close to the rainforest floor, there is hardly any wind. For many plants, this is how they are pollinated, here however, this is mainly done by insects, of which there are countless in the rainforest—and also mammals. They carry the pollen from flower to flower and place to place and thus help the plant to reproduce. Some animals also eat the plants and then their droppings spread the seeds around! Through their colors (and often their smell), the plants attract the animals.

Gloriosa lily can grow up to 2 m (6.5 ft) tall.

You can spread the sap of the dragon's blood tree on a wound—then it works like a liquid bandage.

The rainforest as a pharmacy

Many remedies or their ingredients were discovered in the rainforest. Long before modern research, indigenous peoples accumulated a great deal of knowledge about plants and their effects. The grated bark of a tree they call monguenza can help against fever. The sap of other plants can act as a disinfectant or help against coughs.

19

Water, Swamps, and Healthy Mud

Bays are clearings in the African rainforest. Even from a distance, you can hear that these clearings are meeting places for animals such as the forest elephant. Their rumblings and trumpetings echo deep into the jungle...

Nourishing mud

What make the bays so special? The minerals that lie in the mud! Forest elephants bore holes in it with their trunks, suck out the mud, and stick it in their mouths. The minerals are important nutrients.

Bays are swampy, grassy areas that contain a large variety of ferns and plants that float in the water.

Pygmy hippos are about 1.5 m (5 ft) long and 76 cm (2.5 ft) tall.

Pygmy hippos

These hippos weigh up to 250 kg (550 lbs) and are lightweights compared to their relatives, the large hippos—they can weigh over 2700 kg (6000 lbs)! Pygmy hippos are solitary animals that like to spend time in the water. On land, they sleep a lot. Hippos are able to protect themselves from the sun with special glands in their bodies that secrete a substance that protects their skin. Because this mucus is red, hippos used to be thought to sweat blood.

Elephants use their tusks
as tools to dig up roots
or shave the bark from trees.

Four-legged rainforest gardeners

Bays are important places for forest elephants. Here they find food and also meet up with other elephants. In their search for food, they may cover many miles a day, and in doing so they often trample down bushes, scatter seeds, and strip the bark off trees. This enables other vegetarian animals such as gorillas to gain access to important minerals that lie hidden in the earth. The paths that they carve out through the jungle are also useful to other inhabitants of the rainforest.

When they dive, pygmy hippos close their ears and nostrils so that water can't get in!

21

Our Relatives in the Jungle

The rainforest is home to tiny primates like the pygmy marmoset, which only weighs about five ounces, and to orangutans and gorillas, which are real giants, weighing in at around 226 kg (500 lbs).

Primates

Primates include many different animals—for example anthropoids (animals that resemble human beings) like gorillas, chimpanzees, and orangutans. Lemurs, tarsiers, gibbons and baboons are also primates. Like us, they have fingerprints by which they be individually identified.

They have comparatively large brains, and they use tools to help in the search for food. Many of them even deliberately eat medicinal plants when they're ill, and we can use their knowledge in our own development of medicines.

De Brazza's monkeys have a white beard that makes them look like an old wizard. They store the food they forage in cheek pouches and are very good swimmers, which is quite unusual for primates!

Typical features of the **mandrill** are the brightly shining face and the colourful bottom. In the highest ranking males, the colours are especially vivid. They use their long canine teeth to defend their horde, and they are social and intelligent.

Gorillas are extremely intelligent animals. Their family groups are led by the oldest males. Gorillas generally move on all fours, but sometimes they rear up in order to fight or to beat their chests as a means of frightening others away.

With their silky fur, black faces and funny hairstyles, **colobus monkeys** are especially pretty. They live high in the trees in large groups, and feed mainly on leaves.

Orangutans spend most of their lives in trees, where they build nests of leaves and branches—one for the day and one to sleep in.

Chimpanzees are one of our closest relatives. They are very intelligent, they laugh and play, they can recognize themselves in the mirror, and use tools.

A Kingdom of its Own

Off the east coast of Africa lies an island which is home to many species that are only to be found there and nowhere else in the world. The name of the island is Madagascar.

A unique island

Madagascar was separated from the African continent more than a hundred million years ago, and over this long period of time, Nature has evolved in its own unique way. Plants and animals (like lemurs and fossas) that only exist in one place are called endemics. Madagascar's past animals were also amazing: in former times the largest bird in the world lived here—the elephant bird, which weighed up to 1,100 pounds.

Lemurs are part of the primate family—there are and there more than a hundred species of lemur! They are thought to be the worlds oldest primates.

Fossas can grow up to 32 inches long, and look rather like cougars. They are the largest predators on Madagascar.

?

Size:
226,700 sq miles

Unique feature:
It was one of the last places on Earth to be inhabited.

Unique animals:
Fossa, lemur, mouse lemur, hedgehog tenrec, red tomato frog

Unique plants:
Darwin's orchid, African monkey-bread tree, dragon's blood tree.

Multiskilled

Chameleons are famous for their ability to change colour. Many turn black when they're afraid. Under stress they shimmer in bright tones, and they are especially colourful when they're looking for a mate. Chameleons have one of the finest hunting weapons Nature ever invented: their sticky tongue, which shoots out at lightning speed to grab their prey. Their eyes can move independently of one another, enabling them to see all their surroundings at the same time.

Of the 200 known species of **chameleon**, 80 live on Madagascar.

The great creepy-crawlies

Almost a quarter of known animal species worldwide are beetles of one sort or another.
They protect their sensitive hind wings with solid wing cases. Many beetles are fine athletes: they sprint through the bushes, burrow into the earth, and can even swim. More than 20,000 different kinds of beetle have been discovered so far on Madagascar—most of them endemic, i.e. unique to the island. There are also 1,300 different kinds of bug, 76 species of dragonfly, and hundreds of different biting flies and mosquitoes.

Madagascar is home to about 400 varieties of spider, which include some very specialized hunters, such as Nephila konaci, whose web can have a diameter of more than three feet. The *nephila konaci* is the biggest web-spinning spider in the world. The legs of the female can be as long as 12 cm (5 in), and her body is 4 cm (1.5 in) wide. The males are about five times smaller.

The Asian Rainforest

The Asian rainforest, which is one of the most humid biomes in the world, stretches across several states and islands. No wonder, with so much water from the Indian and Pacific Oceans!

Borneo is the third largest island in the world after Greenland and New Guinea.

Bornean Rainforest

Scientists have so far found 15,000 varieties of plants on this large island—that's five times more than in the whole of Germany. And every year they discover new ones. The density of the rainforest, and the teeming life that inhabits it, can be gauged from the following statistics: 221 species of mammals, 400 of reptiles and amphibians, and about 620 of birds.

The river Kapuas is the longest in Borneo. Because of the warm climate and the abundance of food, most fish breed here throughout the year. These include havel and **kissing gurami**.

In 2005, a new species of animal was found on Borneo which appears to exist only in the river Kapuas: the **Kapuas mud snake**. It is venomous and, just like the chameleon, it can change its colour.

The peat bog forests of Borneo are gigantic stores of CO_2 and can hold between 3,000 and 6,000 tonnes of carbon per hectare— about 50 times as much as similar rain forests without peat bogs. They are therefore very important for the Earth's climate.

Volcanoes

Indonesia is an island country with almost 130 active volcanoes, including Mount Kerinci (3800 m or 12,484 ft high) in the Kerinci-Seblat National Park on the island of Sumatra. A volcano is regarded as extinct if it has not been active for 10,000 years. If there have been no eruptions for a long period, it is regarded as dormant but capable of becoming active at any time.

Thanks to their special claws, bats can hang head downwards without using any muscle power. The weight of their bodies automatically tightens the grip of their claws.

Batcave?

Borneo has the largest known cave system in the world. Approximately two million bats live in Deer Cave alone. These colonies produce huge amounts of bat guano (poo!) which provides food for many of the small inhabitants of the caves.

Close to the exit, there is a rock formation that resembles the profile of the 16th American President Abraham Lincoln. But he himself never saw it!

Survival

In order to get enough food, plants and animals have developed extraordinary abilities or have cooperated as partners.

Orchids already existed during the time of the dinosaurs—a piece of amber from the time was found that contained a bee with orchid pollen.

What's that smell?!

Many flowers smell sweet, but some stink. Both use their scent as a strategy for survival. Very few rainforest flowers can compete with the titan arum for height—it can reach over 3 m (10 ft)—or for stink! It smells like rotten meat. But this attracts beetles, and in return they take charge of pollination.

Ant plants

You might wonder how ants and plants work as a community—they are so different! But that is precisely why they help each other. Ants live in cavities of the roots, feeding on the nectar of the plant, and in return, they protect the plant from other insects that may harm it.

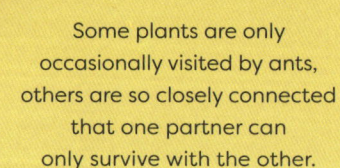

Some plants are only occasionally visited by ants, others are so closely connected that one partner can only survive with the other.

Small aviators

This survival artist reaches just 10 cm (4 in) in length **Wallace's flying frog** can glide up to 15 m (50 ft) through the air from one branch to another, which is a great help in escaping from predators. The membranes between its toes act like parachutes. **Draco lizards** (also called flying dragons) are also skilful gliders. They use flight membranes on both sides of their bodies.

Komodo dragons live on the Indonesian island of Komodo and some of the neighbouring islands.

Scaly scares

Very few creatures survive a meeting with either of these two dangerous giants. The **Komodo dragon** is the largest lizard in the world and is strong enough to knock down and eat a fully grown water buffalo. Its saliva contains venom, and its teeth are razor sharp. The **king cobra**, with a length of up to 3.6 m (12 ft), is the longest poisonous snake in the world. They feed on lizards and other kinds of snake, and are immune to their venom! They do not hiss like other snakes but make a sort of grumpy, growling, grumbling sound.

One bite from a **king cobra** is enough to kill an elephant.

Animals and Plants in the Asian Rainforest

Life in the rainforest is uniquely fascinating. Among other things that Emma and Louis encounter are a giant stinker, a rare ungulate (animal with hooves), and one of the oldest plants in the world.

Ferns

Ferns are easy to recognize because of their feathery fronds. They propagate by forming countless tiny spores. Mayferns grow on the ground, but some also grow on trees, where they get more sunlight.

Ferns have been in existence for 400 million years.

The wide pads of the tiger's paws enable it to move very quietly.

Sumatran tiger

The Sumatran tiger's stripes provide it with perfect camouflage in the alternating light and shade of the rainforest. This enables them to creep up unnoticed on their prey. When tigers run or lie down, their claws retract, but they automatically come out when the tiger pounces on its prey.

There are only a few hundred of these tigers still living on the Indonesian island of Sumatra. That is why their protection is especially important.

Saolas

These rare ungulates are also known as spindlehorns. Their discovery in 1993 was a sensation—most scientists were convinced at that time that all the large rainforest mammals had already been discovered. As saolas are so rare and therefore so difficult to observe, little is known about them.

Southern Cassowary

These giants are running birds. They can't fly, but they are very fast movers. Their sharp claws help to defend them against predators. They can grow up to 1.8 m (6 ft).

The giant rafflesia is the biggest flower in the world sometimes growing to over 100 cm (40 in) in diameter!

Rafflesias

Rafflesias are parasitic flowers—they depend on other plants to keep them alive. They do this by extracting essential nutrients from their hosts. When the flowers open, they stink like rotten meat, and this attracts flies which carry the pollen to other rafflesias. The flowers die after just a few days, and it can take up to nine months before they blossom again.

Amazing Partners

At first sight you often can't tell that two different forms of life depend on each other. This is called symbiosis, and it's quite common in the rainforests.

What is symbiosis?

Symbiosis means "living together", in the sense that both partners benefit from each other. Sometimes they can also live separately, and so the partnership is only occasional and doesn't last. But there are also partners that can only survive if they stay together.

Tualang trees and giant bees

The tualang tree can grow to a height of 250 feet and is one of the tallest trees in Asia. It's also home to the biggest honey bees in the world. The open hives, made from branches and stalks, look like walls. That is why the tualang is also known as the bee tree. The tree provides a home for the bees, and the pees pollinate the tree.

The leaves of the bromeliad are bright green, pink or yellow.

What is a parasite?

When one species exploits another, we call it a parasite. It extracts nutrients from the other, and damages it in the process. Many parasites, such as worms, eat the inside of the host, while others (e.g. ticks and fleas) damage the outside.

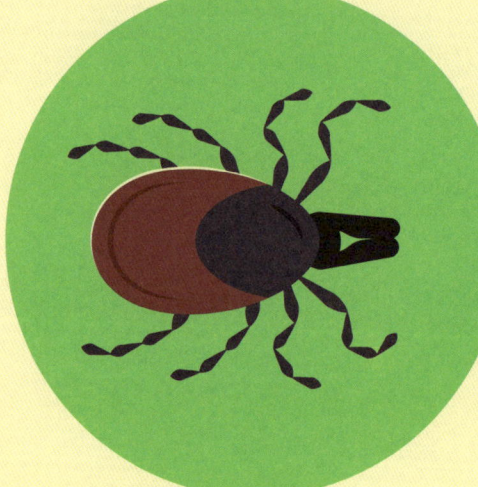

Pitcher plants and treeshrews

Pitcher plants are carnivorous (meat-eating) plants that feed on insects. Treeshrews are their partners. The treeshrews lick the sweet juice from the lid of the plant, which makes them do a poo. This is good for the plant because it contains important nutrients, and so treeshrew droppings fertilize the pitcher.

Hummingbirds and Heliconia

Heliconias are mainly pollinated by certain kinds of hummingbirds. The curved beak of the hummingbird fits perfectly into the curved flower. The bird likes the taste of the nectar.

There are three basic types of symbiotic relationships:

mutualism (where both organisms benefit—like the hummingbird and the heliconias), **commensalism** (where neither organism is harmed but one of them benefits—like the bromeliad crabs) and **parasitism** (where one benefits but the other is harmed—like worms or fleas).

Bromelie & Bromeliad Crabs

The bromeliad crab lives its entire life in the small pools of water that collect in the leaves. They collect food from the leaves and even clear out the dead leaves that fall into their nests.

Up in the Air

More than a thousand varieties of bird live in the rainforest. Many have especially shiny feathers and amazingly powerful beaks, and perform highly individual dances!

Raggiana bird of paradise

The male has gorgeous feathers and performs a special courtship dance in order to impress the female. He even bows to her! By spreading out his feathers, he tries to show her what a fine, fit partner he would be.

Fruit doves

The name tells us what they eat. Fruit doves live in the treetops, where they find plenty of food. The bright feathers act as camouflage between the blossoms and the fruit.

Not all birds live up in the trees—some of them live on the ground!

Rhino birds

The beak of the rhino bird is quite big but also light. Its edges are serrated, which enabled the bird to saw open the hard shells of some fruits. There are about 50 species of rhino bird. They live in pairs, often in large communities and in the vicinity of monkeys. The monkeys brush off insects, thus providing the birds with a nice, easy meal.

Rhino birds can live as long as forty years.

Each rhino bird has a unique beak with its own pattern—the equivalent of our fingerprints.

The **harpy eagle** is one of the strongest birds of prey in the world. Its claws are bigger than a bear's paws, and it can snatch monkeys and sloths from a branch and carry them away.

The **tawny frogmouth** generally hide during the day. They hunt at night and catch insects with their broad beaks.

Mangrove Forests

Mangroves are various bushes and trees that flourish particularly in salt water on the coast or at the mouth of a river.

Where the Amazon flows into the Atlantic, there are huge mangrove forests. They are a wild jungle of overgrown bushes and trees, mud, and swamp.

Important Roots

The roots of the mangrove filter the salt from the seawater before the trees can absorb it. When the tide comes in, you can't see the great tangle of roots, but when it goes out, the trees look as if they are standing on stilts. The roots are not just supports for the trees but are also home to many forms of life, including fish, shrimps, and reptiles. Higher up, there are mammals such as sloths and all kinds of birds which look for worms and mussels when the tide is out. Every few months the trees are hosts to other visitors, as migratory birds like to break their long journeys by taking a rest in the mangrove forests.

Mudskippers

Mudskippers are fish that live out of the water. They store water in their mouths and gills so that they can breathe.

Giant Grouper Fish

A predatory fish which spends a long time at nursery school among the mangrove roots. Only after six years, when it's about 90 cm (3 ft) long, does it leave this habitat and swim out into the open sea where it will continue to grow.

Mangroves breathe through aerial roots, which have large pores that enable them to absorb oxygen. Sometimes these breathing roots look like pencils sticking out of the water.

Pistol Shrimp

This little shrimp lives in deeper waters. It uses its pincers to fire bubbles into its prey at a speed of over 96km/h (60mph). A single blow will paralyse or kill the victim!

Indigenous Groups in Asia

The indigenous people of the rainforest, who have stuck to their traditions, have special knowledge of their own. On a visit to the Korowai, Emma and Louis learn how houses can be built in trees, without any drawings or construction plans.

Houses in the treetops

The Korowai, who follow the traditions of their ancestors, don't build villages or settlements. The families live in tree houses made of bark, branches, lianas and palm leaves, and about 30 m (100 ft) above the ground! They don't use nails or ropes—the lianas bind the different sections together. You need not only special knowledge to build such houses, but also a highly advanced ability to climb and to keep your balance if you are to move around safely at such a height. The Korowai pass their knowledge and skills on orally from one generation to the next.

Why make a home so high up? The height protects families from the animals in the jungle and from floods.

Helping each other

It is part of Korowai culture that families support one another. If a new house is to be built, other families help with the work, even though they won't be living there. But next-door neighbours live a long way away from one another. It takes quite a while to get from one house to another.

The houses last for several years, but the weather erodes them, or insects gnaw away at them, and they gradually become rotten. Then the family will move to another tree and build another house.

All the building materials decompose in time. Then orchids grow again on the branches, and lianas stretch over them—the jungle reclaims its property.

Mealtime with the Korowai

Wild boar, snakes, spiders, birds, frogs, and small marsupials are all items on the Korowai menu, along with palm leaves and fern tips. The cooking is done on a fireplace on the floor of the tree house, and this is contained within a protective wall of clay and leaves to stop the fire from spreading.

The Korowai hunt with stone axes and knives made from bones.

The Korowai dig pits to trap the animals they want to eat.

South American Rainforest

The Amazon rainforest is the largest in the world. A thousand rivers flow through it, including one of the longest in the world—the Amazon itself.

Record breaking rainforest

The South American rainforest stretches out across Brazil, French Guiana, Suriname, Guyana, Venezuela, Ecuador, Peru, and Bolivia. The largest section is in Brazil, and its surface covers an area larger than the whole of western Europe. Over a square mile you will find up to a thousand different trees. You will also hear the sound of a huge natural orchestra: monkey screeches harmonize with insect chirrups and a vast variety of birdsongs, and the rushing waters of the Amazon provide the background music. The river itself is not only thousands of miles long, but in some places is well over 91 m (300 ft) deep.

For about 40km (25 miles) out to sea, one can still bathe in freshwater.

The most powerful river on earth

For several months in the year, the rain is particularly heavy. Then the Amazon bursts its banks and floods far into the rainforest. At the point where it flows into the Atlantic, it is over 240km (150 miles) wide. So much freshwater enters the sea here that it would fill a million bathtubs!

Size:
2,124 million square miles.

Unique feature:
There are many indigenous groups in South America. In Brazil, for example, there are 500,000 indigenous people belonging to 208 groups, such as the Guarani and the Kaingang. There are also uncontacted groups, such as the Kawahiva.

Unique animals:
river dolphin, tapir, giant otter, jaguar, arowana, cassowary

Unique plants:
Special plants: cocoa tree, Brazil nut tree, rubber tree.

Long before Christopher Columbus arrived in South America, people lived in the rainforest around the Amazon. They built settlements, roads and temples.

Amazon river dolphin

The Amazon river dolphin is the largest freshwater dolphin—as well as the smartest! Adult males are the pinkest in colour and they can live to be up to 30 years old.

Some scientists think that only half of all animal, plant and fungus species on earth have been researched.

Dangerous Plants

Many plants may look pretty but they can also be dangerous. Some have slippery mouths or even sticky tentacles to catch their prey!

Up in the air

Lianas grow from the floor of the forest and spread in all directions, using other plants in order to climb—which they do to heights of up to 1000 feet. They are woody climbers which only occur in rainforests and are among the fastest growing of all plants.

> Lianas (vines) can be 70 m long! Many animals use them to climb along them.

Carnivorous plants

We take it for granted that animals eat plants, but sometimes the process is reversed. Some plants eat animals—mainly insects. Although there is plenty of light and water in the jungle, there are not many nutrients in the soil. And so carnivorous plants draaw their nutrients by digesting insects. Some of them even eat small mammals, which they attract with their scent.

Sundew

The red hairs on its leaves look beautiful, but hanging on their tips are transparent, sticky droplets. When an insect lands on these, it can't get away. The sundew rolls up its leaves and eats the insect.

Venus Flytrap

The venus flytrap is another meat-eater. The hairs on its petals are tentacles. As soon as an insect lands in the trap, the leaves close and the prey is digested.

Is there space for me?

Orchids, bromeliads, and some cacti, ferns and lichens are classified as epiphytes—plants that grow on other plants. This enables them to get more sunlight.

Epiphytes (sometimes called air plants) do not need soil and can simply grow on top of the branches.

The strangler fig's roots that are wrapped around another tree look like a skeleton!

Danger!

The strangler fig starts its life as an epiphyte at the top of a tree. From up there it gradually produces long aerial roots which cling to the bearer tree as they push downwards, When they reach the ground, they force their way into the soil and in time grow longer and thicker. The strangler fig now becomes a parasite. Its roots twine themselves round the base of the tree like a net and cut off the host's supply of nutrients and water. The tree dies and eventually disintegrates. All that remains is a strangler fig tree.

Jungle Camouflage

Some animals can hardly be seen among the bushes, lianas and foliage. The colours and patterns of their fur or their amazing behaviour can help them to blend in with their surroundings.

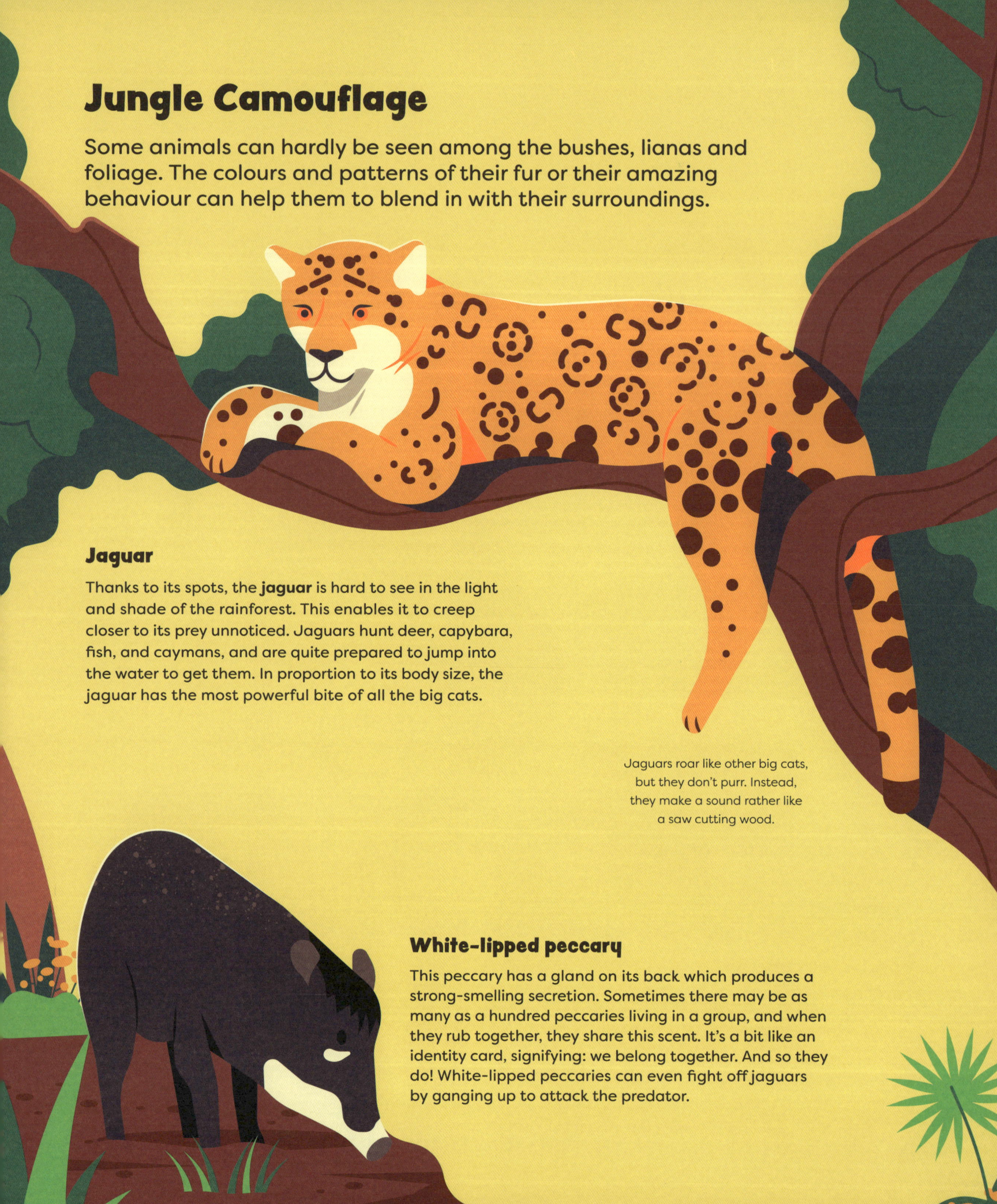

Jaguar

Thanks to its spots, the **jaguar** is hard to see in the light and shade of the rainforest. This enables it to creep closer to its prey unnoticed. Jaguars hunt deer, capybara, fish, and caymans, and are quite prepared to jump into the water to get them. In proportion to its body size, the jaguar has the most powerful bite of all the big cats.

Jaguars roar like other big cats, but they don't purr. Instead, they make a sound rather like a saw cutting wood.

White-lipped peccary

This peccary has a gland on its back which produces a strong-smelling secretion. Sometimes there may be as many as a hundred peccaries living in a group, and when they rub together, they share this scent. It's a bit like an identity card, signifying: we belong together. And so they do! White-lipped peccaries can even fight off jaguars by ganging up to attack the predator.

This is a good way to relax!

Sloth

Algae grow on their fur, giving it a greenish tinge. The sloth provides good living quarters for algae, as its dry skin, fat and hair provide nutrients. Sloths have an unfair reputation for being lazy, In fact, their slow movements simply save energy, and because they move so slowly, predators such as birds of prey often fail even to notice them.

The banana plant can grow to a height of up to thirty feet, and its flowers attract hummingbirds and butterflies. It is also pollinated by flying foxes and bats.

45

Little Insects Think Big

There were insects on Earth as long as 400 million years ago. They have amazing abilities to adapt themselves to changing climates and environments.

Leafcutter ants

Using their mouths as tools, these ants cut up the leaves and use them as material in their underground nests so that a certain spongy fungus can grow there. Just like farmers, the ants lay it all out in fields, which create a process of symbiosis: the ants themselves produce a kind of antibiotic which protects the fungus, and by cultivating the fungus they provide themselves with essential nutrients.

Leaf cutter ants are extremely well organized. They have a queen, soldiers, scouts and different kinds of workers. Each ant knows what job it has to do.

24-hour-ant

Look out! Before it attacks, this large ant emits a stinking fluid and makes a squeaky sound. Also known as the bullet ant, Its bite is said to be one of the most painful of all insect bites—but its venom has no lasting effects after 24 hours.

Over a million different species of insects have been discovered up to now. But it's estimated that there could be ten times as many.

Praying Mantis

When a praying mantis is lying in wait, she folds her front catching legs in front of her chest in such a way that it looks as if she's praying. She can sit there for hours without moving. But she snaps up prey such as bees, spiders, and even frogs and small birds at lightning speed. Some praying mantises can grow up to 6 inches. When they're hungry, the females can also eat the males—sometimes after and sometimes even before mating.

Praying mantises have thorns on their front legs. Any prey has virtually no chance of getting away.

Young giant leaf insects are also brown, and look like mossy twigs. They spend most of their time sitting motionless on branches or leaves.

The walking leaf is another insect that can sit still for hours on end. It looks exactly like a leaf, and this protects it from predators. It only becomes active at night.

? Most members of the animal kingdom are not vertebrates and have no internal skeleton. Insects are among them.

The titan beetle (a giant longhorn beetle) is one of the largest known beetles and can grow up to 16.7 cm (6.6 in). Its jaws are so powerful that they can bite through a pencil. The larvae feed on wood and live underground.

47

To the Water

Riverbanks in the rainforest are surrounded by lianas and colourful flowers. The waters of the Amazon and its tributaries attract animals to come and drink—and also animals which come as hunters in search of prey.

Tapir

Tapirs are usually loners and creatures of habit. They always follow the same tracks through the dense forest, and in time these become well trodden paths which make it easier for them to move from one place to another. They are good swimmers and use their trunks as snorkels as well as to pluck tasty leaves from plants and trees.

Capybara

The capybara is the largest rodent in the world. It is closely related to the guinea pig, and can run, swim, dive, and even bark. It eats grass and its own poo—that sounds weird, but it aids the digestion.

Piranhas

With their sharp teeth, piranhas are predators that can tear lumps of flesh out of their victims with a single bite. They live in large shoals, and they fulfil an important function by eating dead or sick animals, thus preventing the spread of disease. They can be a threat to caymans, large predator fish and even their own kind.

Anaconda

These are among the most impressive snakes in the world: the large anaconda is incredibly strong, heavy and long. It can survive without food for months, but when it goes hunting, it uses its huge jaws to grasp its victim as it winds its body round the latter. It can also hunt in water.

In time, white star flowers grow between leaves around the bright red petals of the hot lips plant. These are pollinated by hummingbirds and butterflies

49

Indigenous people in South America

On their tour of discovery, Emma and Louis learn about people who live completely detached from the outside world. One of these groups is the Kawahiva, about whom virtually nothing is known because they don't like having visitors.

No contact

There are indigenous people who don't want any contact with other humans at all but prefer to keep themselves to themselves. These are called "uncontacted" people. Photos and films of them are very rare. The Kawahiva, who live in the Brazilian section of the Amazon rainforest, remain uncontacted so that they can go on living there in peace.

It is believed that the majority of the world's uncontacted people live in South America. They are probably all hunter gatherers, and many of them cultivate and eat crops like cassavas, papayas, and bananas.

Reasons to stay away

The world only got to know about the existence of indigenous people when scientists observed them from the air. These scientists respected the fact that the people did not want any contact with the outside world—for instance, because they wanted to protect themselves against diseases. Living in such remote places—whether in the jungles of South America or on an island in the Indian Ocean—meant that they would be very vulnerable to diseases against which they had developed no immunity.

Many indigenous people use symbols to show that they do not want contact—for instance, by laying crossed arrows on the ground.

Some groups, however, do want contact, so that they can have some influence on important political matters. The Kichwa in Ecuador live in the middle of the Amazon rainforest, where there are large reserves of oil. The Kichwa vehemently oppose exploitation of this resource, because they have lived in harmony with Nature for hundreds of years and they want the rain-forest to remain just as it has always been.

51

Threats to the rainforest

On our journey we have got to know a huge variety of animals and plants, but many of these are now threatened by us humans. What exactly is the threat?

Deforestation

The surface area of the rainforests worldwide is constantly shrinking because of tree felling and fires. Every minute of every day, huge areas the size of several football pitches are being cleared. This endangers the whole range of animals and plants—but it also has consequences for the whole human race. Clearing the forests releases vast quantities of carbon, which in the form of carbon dioxide (CO_2) is a major factor in global warming.

Palm oil

Palm oil is an ingredient of many foods such as margarine, chocolate cream, biscuits and frozen pizzas. Food producers use vast quantities of palm oil because it is cheap, and because oil-bearing palm trees are more fertile than other sources such as rapeseed and soya. Oil palms need a tropical climate, and so they grow best in rainforests. The result is that huge areas are cleared in order to make way for their cultivation.

Tropical wood

Much of the wood we use (e.g. mahogany, teak and jacaranda) comes from rainforest trees that have taken centuries to grow. The wood is commonly used to make furniture and window frames. The industry requires sawmills, lumber yards, and roads, all of which lead to the felling of yet more trees.

Meat production

We humans want to pay as little as possible for the meat we eat. This means getting animals to grow more quickly, and this can be done by feeding them on protein-rich turbo food made from soya. Large areas of rainforest are being cleared just for the production of soya.

Try using re-usables whenever you can! Every little thing helps the environment.

Aluminium

You will find aluminium in packets of chewing gum, tin foil, the lids of yogurt tubs, cans of drink and even many deodorants. The raw material from which aluminium is made is an ore called bauxite. 90% of the world's bauxite is to be found in the tropical landscapes around the equator. Huge areas of the rainforest have to be cleared in order to get at it and to process it.

Time to go home!

What an adventure! During their journey through the rainforests, Emma and Louis have explored three continents. They have discovered new species of animals, found plants with extraordinary abilities, and got to know men, women, and children who live in the rainforest.

In the course of their expedition, Emma and Louis have also learnt about fruits and herbs that have originally come from the rainforests and now form part of our everyday lives—and some of the plants also have medicinal powers.

Something else they have learnt is the fact that there's a great deal we still don't know about the rainforests.

Scientists believe that there are lots of animals and plants we still haven't discovered. The search for new things in our world is far from finished! What matters most, though, is that all of us should protect the rainforests—and that is probably the most important thing Emma and Louis have learnt. We can all help to do this. The rainforests affect the lives of us all, no matter how far away from them we may live, because the climate of the whole world depends on what happens to them.

Glossary

Amphibian
Vertebrates like frogs, toads, and salamanders that mostly live in the water while they are young and breathe through gills, but as adults live on land.

Bacteria
Tiny organisms that consist of a single cell without a nucleus.

Bird
A vertebrate with wings, beak, and two legs. Unlike mammals, which give birth to live babies, birds lay eggs.

Carbon dioxide (CO_2)
A gas which is contained in the air and which collects in large quantities in the Earth's atmosphere through the burning of fossil fuels such as oil, and coal. This changes the climate.

Carrion
The rotting remains of a dead animal.

Christopher Columbus
Famous Italian explorer who sailed from Europe to the American continent in 1492.

Climate
The normal weather in a region, which may be hot or cold, wet or dry, and which will depend on its distance from the equator (near the equator is hot and moist).

Colony
Species, especially birds and insects, that live in groups.

Courtship
The behaviour of birds during the mating season.

Endemic
Only to be found in one place.

Equator
An imaginary line round the centre of the Earth, dividing it into two: the north and south hemispheres.

Evaporation
The transformation of liquid material into gas.

Extinct species
A plant or animal that no longer exists.

Fertilization
The process by which male and female germ cells merge to produce offspring.

Gills
Organs with which marine creatures "breathe" in oxygen from the water.

Habitat
The surroundings in which an organism or group of organisms lives.

Immunity
The body's natural defence against bacteria and viruses that can make us ill.

Indigenous people
The descendants of the original inhabitants of a region ("indigenous" means born there). They have their own languages, communities, and cultures.

Insects
invertebrates with six feet, three body sections, and often two pairs of wings.

Invertebrates
Organisms which do not have a spine, e.g. insects, spiders, and worms.

Larva
The early stage of life for a species that hatches from an egg and undergoes a transformation, e.g. from a caterpillar into a butterfly.

Lianas
Woody vines that start at ground level then spread from tree to tree climbing up to the canopy to try and get as much light as possible.

Mammals
Warm-blooded vertebrates with a steady body temperature, mostly with fur and feeding their young with milk.

Mating season
The period when the male bird or animal is looking for a female partner.

Metabolism
A chemical process by which food is changed into energy and new cells.

Nectar
A sugary solution which is produced by flowers and attracts different members of the animal kingdom.

Nutrient
Materials such as minerals, vitamins, carbohydrates, fats, and proteins which are essential for the growth and survival of all organisms.

Omnivore
An animal that eats plants and meat.

Oxygen
A gas contained in the air, essential for most forms of life.

Parasite plants
They take all or some of their nutrients from other plants (such as fungi), which are called hosts.

Plant
A living thing that has roots, a stem and leaves, and whose metabolism is called photosynthesis.

Pollen
Tiny grains of flower dust which are carried from one flower to another.

Pollination
The transfer of pollen from one plant to another so that the receiver can produce seeds.

Propagation
The process by which plants reproduce themselves.

Reptiles
Vertebrates such as lizards, snakes, tortoises, and crocodiles, which generally live on land and have scales instead of feathers or hair.

Rosette
Leaves of a plant that are tightly packed together.

Spores
Ferns develop these cells instead of seeds for propagation.

Tentacles
Long, movable limbs with which some animals and plants generally catch their prey.

Tides
The flood tide brings the sea water towards the land, and the ebb tide takes it away again. This movement is caused by the moon, which pulls or pushes the water, depending on how close it is to the Earth.

Vertebrates Organisms which have a backbone, e.g. fish, amphibians, reptiles, birds, and mammals.

Explore the Rainforest
Emma and Louis in the Jungle

Written by Anne Ameri-Siemens
Illustrated by Anton Hallmann

This book was conceived, edited,
and designed by Little Gestalten.

Edited by Robert Klanten,
Maria-Elisabeth Niebius and Fay Evans

Translation from German by David Wilson
Design and layout by Anton Hallmann
Typefaces: Filson Soft by Olivier Gourvat
Peachy Keen JF by Jason Walcott

Printed by Schleunungdruck GmbH, Marktheidenfeld
Made in Germany

Published by Little Gestalten, Berlin 2022
ISBN 978-3-96704-719-6

For more information, and to order books, please visit
www.little.gestalten.com

Bibliographic information published by the Deutsche Nationalbibliothek.
The Deutsche Nationalbibliothek lists this publication in the Deutsche
Nationalbibliografie; detailed bibliographic data are available online at
www.dnb.de

Anne Ameri-Siemens is an award-winning writer who tells whimsical stories about the world around us. Anne lives in Berlin, but would like to spend more time in the rainforest. This is her second book with Little Gestalten.

Anton Hallmann was born in Brandenburg and studied illustration at the Hamburg University of Applied Sciences. He currently lives in Stockholm with his wife and their bunnies. After *Explore the World,* this is his second children's book.